CEYLON

ISLAND OF GEMS

CEYLON

ISLAND OF GEMS

ELIE L. MENASCHE

GYAN

Published by

Gyan Publishing House
5, Ansari Road
Daryaganj, New Delhi-110002
Phone: 011-47034999, 9811692060
E-mail: books@gyanbooks.com

Distribution Network
gyanbooks.com
India, USA, Canada, UK, Australia, France

ISBN : 978-81-212-3223-4 (PB)
First Published, Colombo

2nd Impression 2020

Printed at: Gyan Press, Delhi.

Ceylon
Island of gems
Author: Elie L. Menasche

Ceylon..........

Island of Gems

LET us imagine that you have arrived in Colombo Harbour and your whole day will be spent ashore. You want to buy a few presents for your people at home and therefore you take a " look-see " in town.

In this most beautiful and poetic Island, where tourists are always given a hearty smile of welcome, your attention will fall upon a score of sights, entirely new to you and you will very soon feel a keen interest for any subject connected with Ceylon.

It has been said that the Garden of Eden was located in this enchanting Island. I like to believe it is so, and would enjoy looking for proofs. That would be an undertaking as romantic as that of the Hindu Yogi who went in search of the spring of crystal pure water that rose where Rama's arrow fell.

But as to you, such a long search is impossible and you decide to stick to the pavements of the town.

In many shops all kinds of curios, made of ebony or tortoise shell, various articles of silverware, the Kandyan style foremost amongst the various designs, can be admired.

Your surprise knows no bounds when you see the large amount of precious stones displayed in almost every shop and you feel bewildered by the range of colours and hues sparkling on silk or velvet or set in precious metals.

You suddenly remember having heard it said that Ceylon is a country of gems.

Your interest is instantly aroused and your impulse is to handle the gems, examine and admire them. As to buying any, that is a different matter. A certain shyness, timidity or even suspicion, comes over you, with a repetition of "I know nothing about gems."

Quite right. You are not supposed to know even a little about stones, as it is a lifetime study. The gem trade is very often the profession of a family, for several generations, as in my case.

But, really, that much knowledge is not necessary if you intend to buy for one or two hundred rupees of loose stones as a present for your family.

Any jewellery shop in Colombo, however small, can supply your modest needs, provided you use your eyes and select clean and pure semi-precious stones such as moonstones, garnets, amethysts, zircons or various coloured quartz which are plentiful in Ceylon. They are so cheap that their imitations would not be cheaper, and a stone with a small flaw makes no great difference in a price already low enough.

This, even taken by itself, is a point that will allay all your fears of being "taken in." It is forbidden to import imitations into this Island, and in any case, in all fairness to the local gem dealers, no one would willingly try to "palm off" a false stone for a genuine one. Pay attention to the price, and try to check it. Bargaining is a pleasure, but there is no fear of being cheated with an imitation, deliberately.

From three to five rupees per carat buys you a fine red garnet, amethyst, pink and blue spinels or cinnamon stones.

A five or six carat stone would measure about half a square inch and would only cost you from 20 to 25 rupees. This example is a more or less fancyful way of expressing myself, as measurements in inches do not come into the usual way of describing stones, but this is to give you a rough idea of the size you can get for your money. Ten rupees per carat would buy you the very best garnet.

Another semi-precious stone cheap enough to tempt the most modest pocket is the topaze. These vary from dark brown to lighter shades and from pale yellow to "brandy" colour. This is the kind found in Ceylon. They do not belong to the topaze family proper being a kind of quartz called locally "padiam." They are not quite so hard, but most attractive and notably cheaper.

For about 10 rupees per carat, you can buy tourmalines in twelve different shades. This gem is very brilliant, usually clean or flawless and is one of the hardest stones in the semi-precious class. In Ceylon the tourmaline is called the "mother stone." Probably because where tourmalines are found one also finds sapphires and rubies. Sometimes one can see a tourmaline crystallised on "horse back" on top of a corundum—(from which, of course, it has to be cleaved)—Some specimens have two colours clearly defined, being, for instance, half apple green and half pink, but not in the Ceylon kind.

What makes any stone valuable is, first of all, its colour: I mean the *Right* colour among so many different shades.

Secondly, its purity.

Thirdly, its brilliance or lustre.

Then, with all these qualities, its shape and size.

Keep those points in mind when making a selection, and you will get a perfect gem.

Semi-Precious

There are, of course, many other gems, much more costly in spite of their also being called semi-precious. This word means that they are not as rare nor as difficult to obtain as other stones qualified as precious. But such a distinction is quite arbitrary. Fine quality semi-precious stones such as beryls, alexandrites, cats' eyes, spinels, etc., cost much more than a medium quality gem called precious.

As a striking example, I can mention that several years ago, I bought a red spinel, in Burma, for 250 rupees per carat. And I did not take it for a ruby, by mistake, because a ruby of the pigeon blood colour is worth over twenty times that much. And yet, that was a semi-precious stone. However, as this red spinel had almost the right colour of the costly ruby, the price I paid for it was certainly not too high.

I could not have made a mistake and taken it for the much more valuable ruby, even if this spinel had been exactly the same colour. There are two reasons why I could not make this mistake.

First, because the hardness of the ruby is 9, being a corundum and the spinel only 8. So that a ruby can scratch a spinel, but the spinel could not leave a mark on the ruby.

Second, because it has a specific gravity of only about three and a half but for the ruby it is four.

The same two points of comparison can apply to any different gems of the same colour, in order to classify them without possible doubt or mistake. Reds, greens and yellows are colours found in several stones absolutely foreign to each other.

As I am writing these lines, a friend is reading over my shoulder and he advises me to illustrate this point " with some antidote." I realise he means anecdote and I have a typical one to tell you.

A few years ago, on one of the " Franconia's " world tours, I met an American lady who was, it seemed to me, extremely disappointed after her visits to a few jewellery stores in Colombo. She was in search of a fine blue sapphire of about 10 carats and had been unable to find the right colour. I asked her if she had been at such and such store and if she had seen their collection, as well as their specimen qualities, between 200 and 300 rupees per carat.

Yes, she said, she had seen them and found good quality sapphires among them at prices even higher than those mentioned. But, she added, there was not a single one of the colour she was looking for.

I hid a smile. I knew very well that fine corn flower blue sapphires, as well as the deep royal blue shade, were to be found in these collections, and I also felt I knew why *she* could not find them.

In short, she concluded she had given up the idea ever to get one in Ceylon, and she thought it a great pity, as she was passing through the country of origin, and could not find a single stone to her taste.

I surprised her very much when I affirmed that I was positive I had in my stock the very shade of blue she was looking for, and asked her for one hour's time to bring the stone and show it to her. I selected only one gem in my collection. When I showed it to her she seized it eagerly and asked me with a happy smile how I came to guess so well the shade she was looking for. I explained that it is part of my trade to know what the client wants and she bought the stone instantly.

Now here is the explanation. I can give it to my readers, but it might have upset or angered the lady. Hers was a clear case of colour blindness, and I understood it as soon as she started complaining. She had most certainly been shown the very best shades of corn flower blue, but her eyesight being defective, she saw them another shade altogether. Therefore I concluded she must be shown another colour in the ladder of blues and I chose for her a slightly greenish blue, the colour found on some duck's feathers, and to her it was the perfect tint. I sold her a blue spinel.

Now that I have mentioned the sapphire, I will continue on this subject and give you some advice on how to select one when buying. The corundum is the only one family of precious stones, found in Ceylon. Its hardness is second to the diamond only, being 9/10ths. It can cut glass almost as easily, if a sharp edge is used. Its specific gravity is also one of the heaviest, but not *the* heaviest, which is 4.

Some members of this famous family are :—

(1) The red corundum called ruby.

(2) The blue corundum called sapphire.

(3) The purple or violet, called oriental amethyst.

(4) The yellow or golden, called oriental topaze.

(5) A range of hot shades, apricot, orange, pinky or tango called King topaze or King sapphire.

(6) The white, sometimes slightly tinged with yellow or pink, called white sapphire.

Very frequently this variety is cut like a diamond, with 56 facets. Some very fine specimens, exceptionally fine, can be mistaken for diamonds by the public, when properly set, and of course when they are worn by people who could easily afford diamonds . .

The various kinds of corundums have been explained to you, and now you decide to buy a blue sapphire. Keep in mind that there is a ladder of about twenty shades of blue, starting from pale sky blue to deep corn flower. The lightest shades are the cheapest, 20, 30 and 40 rupees a carat, for the first five tints. Prices go up very swiftly as you proceed to the sixth. Let us call it a quarter colour. When you reach the tenth, or half colour, prices may rise from 50 to 150 rupees per carat. From the 11th to the 15th shade, a rich corn flower tint is your reward and we will call it a three-quarter colour. These may be worth from 200 to 300 rupees per carat, and the last five tints, comprising the full rich and deep corn flower blue, may cost you as much as 400 or 500 rupees a carat, if the stone is at least of 10 carats size, which is very rare and most difficult to find.

The right colour is the first thing you want to look for when selecting a blue sapphire. The colour (together with a size of from 8 to 12 carats per stone) is the most important point, as I said before.

To see the exact colour of a stone I advise looking at it in a north light or turning your back to the daylight, so that it reflects into the stone examined. Of course you must remember that colour is usually very deceptive and that is why stones should not be judged by artificial light. Your colour vision must also be correct. I want to mention, and purely as a matter of curiosity, that when viewed in a yellow light, rubies are black and diamonds yellow. Only the white light of the sun can show you tho various grades of colour, provided of course, that your sight is normal.

After colour comes purity; then fire or lustre, finally shape. If these four qualities are in a single sapphire, you have found a perfect blue corundum and 400 to 500 rupees per carat is not too dear. Remember that small diamonds, the size of a pin head, cost 1,000 rupees per carat.

Speaking of prices, I would like to emphasize the fact that a precious stone has no fixed price and those I have mentioned are only given as general indication.

Even gem merchants and jewellers have to pay sometimes a greater price for a quality of stones they had previously obtained at a cheaper rate. The law of offer and demand operates here more than in any other line of business. But what does it matter if sometimes you have to pay a little more as long as the gem is really a good one ? Or if it has rare and peculiar features, such as a blue sapphire with a reddish frame-like mark all round the stone I once bought at a fancy price.

Also some people—you perhaps—may agree to pay more for an article because it is an antique, say about two or three hundred years old. Splendid. Then why not agree to pay a little more for a gem that is no less than 50 million years old, since it belongs to the amazing and wonderful Eretaceous period ? Would you grudge a few rupees more for gems of the Archaean period of a thousand million years ? A gem is an antique.

Look carefully for flaws in the stones.

This is what you must avoid in a sapphire. Defects are of course almost unavoidable in any real gem, but you must eliminate first and foremost a real flaw. That is a black spot or a foreign body embedded in the stone. I call this a real flaw, as compared with others that I call minor defects, such as a scratch or silk.

The scratch, if any, must be deep inside and hardly visible, but never on the surface. And a scratch does not mean that there is a break in the stone. Silk is the visible natural crystallisation of the stone revealing itself by a silver glitter when one looks at the stone at a certain angle. Silk cannot be called a flaw and even less a defect. In fact it is the birth mark, the one hundred per cent. irrefutable proof of genuineness. I even advise you to select a sapphire that *has* silk, as long as it does not run below the surface of the gem, the whole length of it, but is placed in a discreet way, in a corner or on the edge of the stone.

If you find all the qualities I have mentioned in a single ten carat size sapphire, you have selected the very best.

I must, however, emphasize that there are two kinds of purity, one seen with the naked eye, the other with the magnifying glass.

Yet, if I were to buy sapphires with a magnifying glass that would enlarge them 7 or 10 times, I might just as well give up my profession as there is almost no precious stone, of large size, chemically pure.

And in any case one can never demand such perfection for a stone priced only 100 or 200 rupees per carat. If the stone is pure when seen with the naked eye, that is sufficiently rare. The only time when I would use a magnifying glass is when examining a diamond costing 2,000 rupees per carat and weighing one and a half or two carats.

Among the wonderful gems owned by the British Royal Family, the blue sapphire is a favourite. On very special occasions, that exquisite gem comes foremost. Just lately when Princess Elizabeth married, Queen Mary gave the happy royal couple a full set of Ceylon blue sapphires.

A few years ago H.R.H. the Duke of Gloucester presented his bride with a sapphire ring and so did Prince George when he selected Princess Marina's engagement ring. They were blue sapphires from Ceylon, mined in Ratnapura, about 70 miles from Colombo. The best gems are found in the villages around that town. Rakwana is one of these, and even in Paris, I have often heard a perfect blue called Rakwana blue.

It is interesting to note that the name of corundum (for korund) was given to the sapphire family by an English mineralogist as recently as 1798, and his collection of Indian Corundums can be seen, even today, in the British Museum amongst other minerals. He was the Right Honourable Charles Francis Greville.

In September, 1949, a Ceylon newspaper mentioned on its front page, a boxed item of news that surprised a large number of readers. It was to the effect that a corundum of one and a half pound had been found in the pits of Ratnapura. A large number of surprised people came to ask me what I thought about it. I refrained to comment as I did not feel like giving a lecture on the subject.

I wonder what they would have said had I told them that there is a crystal of corundum in the Geological Museum of Pretoria, Transvaal, of a greyish blue, in a perfect hexagonal form and bi-pyramidal (twinned) that measures two feet 3 inches high and 15 inches across and weighs 335 pounds ?

In the British Museum is to be seen a smaller corundum of 34 pounds. But these colossal minerals are not of " gem quality " and would be useless for jewellery.

There are beryls in Madagascar, the size of Greek temple pillars, but the same remark applies.

Some years ago when I was in Burma, I had in my Rangoon office a block of Jade with many different colours, weighing one ton. Alas, there was not a single piece of decent colour big enough to make a tie pin, in the whole mass. Only ash trays could be made with it or small table tops. If the grain is fine, small statues also are carved from these blocks of rock crystal, rose quartz and pale creamy coloured jade. Onyx, calcedony and agate are also carved to make fairly large flower vases, boxes and several curios of large size. Now, here are two more members of the corundum family.

(7) The Star sapphire.

(8) The star ruby.

These two are the most curious and fascinating members, of that family. They are the same as the sapphire or the ruby, but being cloudy and silky with the natural six-angled crystallization clearly visible, they are not translucent. Therefore they are not cut with facets, but polished as cabochons, convex, leaving the silky formation below the stone. The reflection of the sexagonal base gives birth to a star with six rays, a star that you can see playing and moving freely, at any angle, when the gem is moved between the fingers. The star stone is one of the only gems that cannot be imitated perfectly, although many attempts have been made, with mild success. In any case any fraud can be easily detected.

These stones are found in more than fifty different shades, for star sapphires, from white, sky blue to deep royal blue ; for star rubies from light pink violet, purple to deep red.

The lightest shades, in both gems, are the cheapest. Yet, most amazingly, it is in these pale and cheaper qualities that the star is brightest.

A perfect deep blue, or a fine pigeon blood red, very seldom has a strong well defined star. That is the decision you must make when buying such a stone : to choose between the beauty of the star or the depth of the colour. Remember it is hard to find both together.

Because of their high specific gravity, star sapphires weighing five or six carats are no larger than a green pea. Therefore one of ten carats cannot be considered as a large stone and 20 to 30 carat star sapphires are often set in ladies' rings. 10 or 12 carats can easily be set in a man's ring.

The high density of these stones is rather surprising, when we consider that corundum contains mostly the light metal aluminium.

Another peculiarity of sapphires is this : they are nearly always parti-coloured, in blue streaks or patches, sometimes visible to the naked eye, when seen by transparence. It is part of the gem cutter's art to cut the facets of such stones at certain angles so that the colour will be reflected as evenly as possible upon the table of the stone, Some sapphires have one part lighter and one darker. If the contrast between the two is not too striking, it may not be considered a defect. This mixture in shades of the same colour is so natural to the sapphire that imitation try to reproduce it, although clumsily.

The price of a star sapphire varies from Rs. 10 per carat, for the grey, Rs. 20, 30 and 40 for the sky blue and from 50 to 150 rupees per carat for a deep fine blue and a perfect star with six branches. Higher prices, of course, would have to be paid for an exceptionally fine specimen, above ten carats in size.

The price of star rubies is much higher, but they must not be in the purple-violet shades. From clean pink to perfect deep red, prices may range from 60 to 200 rupees per carat and more. A stone altogether perfect in colour, lustre, shape and size is a very rare gem, extremely difficult to find and therefore the extra price one must pay for it is well worth it.

Americans have always shown a great partiality for stars of all shades. Jewellers in Ceylon rarely sell them anything else. America is also the greatest importer of these gems. More than anything else produced here, they have made Ceylon famous in their country.

CHAPTER II

TOURISTS and private buyers are sometimes under the impression that they will meet, on landing in Ceylon, a bunch of local rogues against whom they will have to match their wits. Then there is the type of traveller that pretends to know all about gems and wishes to impress his fellow-passengers. I advise you not to act thus. In a few seconds the dealer will have a good idea of how much you really know : the way you pick up a stone placed in front of you ; the way you extend your hand to receive it, if handed to you ; the way you hold the gem, move it for examination and the way you make use of the light to see the gem clearly and detect defects, are all revealing, as are also the names you will use for the various kinds of flaws. There is also a professional way of taking and holding the pincers, let alone the special technical expressions used in the trade.

I have known merchants with a sense of humour, congratulating warmly such fools, showing a deep amazement for their knowledge, and . . . charging them a good deal more than to clients that simply relied on his professional honesty and on his giving them a fair deal.

Examine the stones over a table or a show case, so that if you drop one it will not be on the cement floor or the pavement, where it may chip off one of its sharp facets. You must never drop a stone, remember that, and handle them carefully.

If you pick it up from the tray, hold it lightly by the back of it, so that you can see the whole surface. Ignorants hold it by the front and hide with their fingers more than half of the gem.

If the stone is offered to you, present the two first fingers of your left hand pressed together and the stone will be placed between these two fingers. You keep your right hand below the left one, in case you should drop the stone through your fingers. You move the two fingers of your left hand that hold the stone very slowly and roll the gem carefully from one angle to another for proper examination and in that way you will easily detect flaws, scratches and silk, provided you examine the stone in strong daylight, preferably north, but not in the sun as it would make you colour-blind for a few minutes.

When asking the price, after examination, make it clear if you want the price per carat or for the whole stone. Get the price in rupees and don't ask how many dollars it amounts to. Don't buy with a suspicious mind, or worry yourself sick over the transaction. Ask advice from disinterested persons, such as your consul or residents.

Don't make up your mind that the bigger the shop, the dearer the goods. That only big jewellers are reliable or that a small shop-owner will sell you for less because he has less overhead expenses. On the contrary he may be more greedy than the owner of the biggest shop. Use your common sense and psychology if you possess enough of it. If not, I repeat it again, ask for reliable advice.

Very often, some passengers, because they are short of time, or careless, or even shy, buy gems from hawkers, guides, or a man they meet at a street corner, or on the pavement while taking a stroll through Colombo.

Most of them had really no intention whatever to buy any stones ashore. Yet, for some sudden and mysterious reason they make a purchase of, say, a hundred rupees. Later, when they are back in their own country and decide to have these stones set, they are told that they are not even worth the cost of a silver setting.

These people, of course, are disappointed, and more especially those who thought that through luck or shrewd judgment they had acquired gems worth very much more in their own country. In their bitter disillusion, they blame their mishap on the whole of Ceylon and give a bad name to this fair Island.

Furthermore, it would be difficult to make these people admit that they were wrong and were paying for their own thoughtlessness. Precious stones should not be bought from a man standing at a petrol station and coming to talk to you while the driver of your taxi gets his tank filled, however cheap they may seem at first sight. Anybody who thinks that in Ceylon they can get something for nothing is mistaken. Here like everywhere you will get a fair deal from the legitimate traders.

If you believe any glib street hawker do not blame anybody else but yourself. Petrol sheds or Resthouses are the wrong places to buy precious stones.

CHAPTER III

AS I have already said if you intend to buy a gem, you need not fear to be cheated with an imitation. No established jeweller could do such a thing and his business survive. In my thirty years experience here, I have not once heard or seen any gem merchant playing such a dirty game with his innocent and gentle buyers. They may have been over-charged, or given a stone containing a flaw, but certainly not a dud. Imitation stones are not allowed in the country as their importation would kill the gem trade of Ceylon, and the customs enforce this rule very strictly.

The gem industry is an important one and so are the numerous trades and professions connected with it. Thousands of goldsmiths, fine metals and tool merchants, crucible manufacturers, die makers, even charcoal dealers and fishermen who supply the gem trade with cuttle fish bone by the ton, this strange porous material being the best to make molds for certain jewels.

But you should, however, be careful when buying a gem. For sometimes it may be misrepresented, the real name not being given. This, I must also say, may be due to ignorance on the seller's part and not to a desire to mislay.

A shop assistant may show you a fine green tourmaline and proudly tell you " This is the Ceylon Emerald." Or show you small and cheap white stones, cut like diamonds, and call them "Rangoon diamonds." They are, of course, not diamonds at all. They were originally cut in Rangoon and now in Madras. Therefore do not get mislaid by names. A spinel ruby is a red spinel. A spinel sapphire is a blue spinel. A ruby garnet is a garnet. This system of naming gems by false analogy is quite illogical. It always leads to misunderstandings and adds necessarily to the burden of the bewildered buyer. Often the merchant himself is as ignorant of the precise name of the gem. A most wonderful solution to this problem was once given by a sceptical mineralogist when in a cynical mood he advised and recommended, in case of doubt, to wear an Amethyst, " which by its charm giveth good understanding of all things that may be misunderstood." Of course, a real expert would laugh when he finds in ancient writings that wearing a sapphire is good for the liver or that some other stone would protect its wearer from fire or burns.

Minerals

The crust of the earth is made up of over one thousand minerals, a hundred of which are more or less precious. Of these, fifty are so rare that it is not worth mentioning them here. For example, torium, uranium, (which are contained in zircons, as a radio active element and that explains the constant molecular changes they suffer). This leaves us with about fifty precious and semi-precious minerals of gem quality, worth being cut and polished. It is the different arrangement of the molecules in these minerals that gives them their different character, easily detectable by their hardness and specific gravity.

As many gems, although totally different, but of the same colour, are often found, they are sometimes mistaken for others and given the wrong name. It is well known that through the ages names have gradually changed in their meaning. A striking example of this is the Black Prince's Ruby, now in the Imperial State Crown of the British Regalia.

That ruby cut as a cabochon (dome shaped and without facets) is said to have been worn by Edward, Prince of Wales at the Battle of Crecy in the year 1346. That red cabochon is of a most irregular shape and still shows indications of its original octahedral form—

that is the twinned crystallisation of the spinel cube. It has also been classified, from one century to another as a carbuncle which is a cabochon garnet. Although called "ruby" for the last six hundred years, its specific gravity and its distinctive crystallisation classifies it definitely and irrefutably as a red spinel, which has no relationship with the sexagonal ruby. Moreover, if analysed, the spinel would be found to be a compound of magnesia iron and chromium, whereas the ruby is an oxide of aluminium. In the olden days, colour was the only criterion and stones were named only according to their colour. One realises what an arbitrary method that was.

The sapphire was originally the name given for Lapis-Lazuli, and the name alcohol was applied by the Arabs to a mineral: al-kohul, the black powder used to darken the eyes and still in use for the stage under the name of kohl. In fact, it is powdered stibrite, an antimony sulphite.

The amethyst being wine coloured, the Greek name for wine was borrowed in its shape of methyl alcohol: Amethustos, which means wine (or methyl) not drinkable. It was, of course, considered a supreme charm against drunkenness or intoxication.

Epsomite is another mineral which is largely supplied nowadays as an imitation and nobody ever complains. Why? Because Epsomite was originally found in 1675 from the bitter springs of Epsom, in Surrey, and known as Epsom salt now manufactured by the ton.

* * * *

Speaking of peculiarities about gems, I wish to recall the subject of a short story written by the French master of short stories, Guy de Maupassant, who is well known to other nations as his works have been translated in practically every language. Although the story appears as his usual fiction, I know it is a true one and has happened many times. In fact, it is because it may happen again—even to you—that I feel it imperative to recall it and warn you at the same time.

In order to attend a ball, a young lady borrowed a diamond necklace from one of her friends as she wanted to appear in public to her best advantage. After a whole night of dancing and enjoyment she went home in the early hours of the next morning. When undressing she discovered—to her profound horror—and despair—that the diamond necklace was missing. The most careful search and the most frantic investigations were in vain.

The next few days were for her a frightful nightmare, when she looked for a similar necklace at all the jewellers in town. At last she found one. Alas, the price was very high and one she could not possibly afford. So she borrowed the money from an usurer. Month after month, and year after year she paid over a hundred instalments.

During all these years she must perforce have denied herself all that she could otherwise have afforded. She lived in the most abject poverty, hiding her misery as best she could, and through pride refusing to even meet her friends. A chance encounter with the owner of the necklace and the latter's grave concern at her altered appearance brought the whole story to light.

Her friend was horrified and could only say: "Why did you not tell me? The necklace I lent you was only a good imitation . . ."

*   *   *   *

It sometimes happen that people eating oysters look carefully for pearls not knowing that the oyster that produces pearls is not edible. A cartoon I saw lately is therefore doubly funny to me. It shows an Oyster bar advertising a vacancy. To a man applying for it, the proprietor of the bar says : " We pay no salary, but if you find a pearl it is yours."

Once I mentioned to a client that a garnet he was interested in was " Rs. 25 for the whole stone."

"Do you think," he asked me, "I wanted to buy only half of it ?"

He did not know, of course, that prices are usually quoted by the carat.

*   *   *   *

Would you like some more peculiar information about gems ? and precious stones in general ?

1. The diamond is composed of only one element : carbon, the most common of all.

2. The sapphire and the ruby, extremely heavy stones, are the result of the cristalization of the lightest of all minerals : aluminium.

3. Black Jet is fossilized wood, a form of coal of a million years ago.

4. Amber is a gum of vegetal origin. Sometimes small insects hundreds of centuries old are fossilized and embedded in its resin.

5. Coral and pearls are of animal origin. Coral grows in the sea like a tree.

6. Opals are solidified juices and jellies a million years old.

7. Lightning striking in the desert sand produces a stone of great beauty called silica-glass, often coloured brightly, but not very hard.

8. Meteors falling from comets or other aerial bodies have produced often gems of celestial or meteoric origin.

9. The atom bomb tried in New Mexico in 1945 formed a saucer shaped crater half a mile in diameter covered with jade and

turquoise-coloured silica glass vitrified in the over-heated sand of the desert, but it could hardly be used as gem quality.

10. Some stones such as Zircons are radio active and suffer inside a constant bombardment of atoms.

11. Tourmalines when rubbed or heated develop a positive charge of electricity at one end but not at the other. This gem is very sensitive to slight changes in temperature and is therefore extensively used by submarines for experiments on the depths of seas and oceans.

12. A kind of pearl is sometimes—although rarely-found inside the tusk of Ceylon elephants. A Colombo jeweller, years ago, showed one to the public as a curious occurrence.

13. Gems have often been found hundreds of miles from their mother rock, carried there either by glaciers, rivers or volcanic power.

14. Gems that were once of one specific kind have often re-crystallized into another stone, when new mineral elements came to rest in the crevices that contained them and thus were transmuted into a quite different precious stone.

15. Rutile is a gem twice brighter than a diamond,—and cheap, too. It gave birth to the word "rutilant", for brilliant.

While we are reviewing some peculiar facts about gems, I think the story of the discovery of the largest diamond ever found would prove of interest: The Chief Engineer of the Premier mines near Pretoria, Transvaal, who was to become later Sir Thomas Cullinan, was walking one day, deep in thought from his bungalow to the mines, then newly discovered. He saw a large pebble on the ground and kicked it twice to the foot of a nearby tree, before he carelessly picked it up. It was almost shapeless, except for the bottom which was flat, and one of the sides which showed a smaller flat and slanting portion. The whole thing looked a yellowish white, as dull as a piece of soda. But closer examination, however, soon proved to him that he had found the largest diamond the world ever produced, a piece measuring 4 by 2½ by 2 inches weighing about one and a half pound, being 3 ·106 carats exactly. Diamonds, when rough have eight natural facets and this would have been identified at a glance if it had had such a shape. But most amazingly this lump had only two flat facet. and no sign of the other six that usually complete the octahedron. Therefore it was evident that this piece was only the smaller portion of a much larger crystal for which a frantic search was made but in vain. This piece had most probably been shot up by some volcanic force and the parent piece was probably still lying in " the blue earth " as diamond beds are called, a few miles below the surface.

I was personally present in Mr. Assher's office when the stone was brought to him. Mr. Assher is a cleaver at Amsterdam. I saw him cleave off a whole slice of about half inch in thickness and two and a half inches long which was yellowish, leaving nine-tenth of the stone a perfect blue white. That was just before the first world war. The stone was called " The Cullinan " and later it was cut in about a hundred diamonds of various sizes. Nearly half the lump was given an egg-shape with facets cut all around it. This form is called a briolet. That very briolet is today set in the sceptre of the King of England, held in place by three gold " fleur de lys."

If 96 small diamonds weigh only 7½ carats in all, the nine larger ones weigh each, respectively, 530, 317, 94, 63, 19, 11, 9, 7 and 4½ carats.

The Cullinan was bought by the Transvaal Government and was presented to King Edward VII who ordered it to be cut as it is today, all these stones belonging to the British Regalia.

Other celebrated and historic diamonds such as the Koh-I-Nor, the Star of Russia, Sancy, Orlof, the Regent, etc., are of ancient cut and hardly have any commercial market value today. But the Cullinan is perfect, or rather all the stones that came from it are altogether perfect, because of modern cut.

Van Dyck, the great Flemish painter used a gorgeous and rich deep blue which he prepared himself. It is due to the use of that particular colour that some of his paintings have been identified as his. Even on his death bed, when his faithful pupils begged for the secret, he refused to reveal it. Rubens, his master, just as jealously kept the secret of all the colours which he, himself, crushed and mixed. Powdered gems were in many, so that they did cost much more than their weight in gold.

Today it is firmly believed that the Van Dyck blue was made of finely powdered lapis-lazuli, which in those days was mistakenly called sapphire.

Can Gems Lose Their Colours?

Under certain circumstances, some gems may lose or rather alter their colour. Zircons, for instance, change colour amazingly quickly, although they do not become entirely colourless. Under the rays of a strong sun the colour may fade in 10 or 15 minutes, and even faster if these rays are concentrated by a magnifying glass. However, if those stones were heated afterwards, some would regain their former shade.

Some gems whose colour is considered as too dark can be lightened by fire. The gem is placed among red charcoal for an hour or two, but this must be done with constant supervision, for if the stone has a crack it may be completely ruined.

For instance, amethysts of a sombre and ugly purple can be made paler or given the shade of a golden topaze if they are exposed to X'rays, radium, violet rays or simply the glowing charcoal. The people using this process are, of course, either lapidaries, gemmers or mineralogists. It might otherwise be a costly and dangerous game for an amateur.

Improving the Colour

Some years ago, a Colombo gem merchant had a perfect star ruby of about 20 carats, but its shade was a dull violet of medium value. Because of its purity and the perfection of its shape, he resolved to improve the colour by the fire process. As the ruby and the sapphire are, in fact, the same stone, being both corundums, this purple shade was the result of both blue and red being present and mixed in that one stone.

That lapidary must have known through previous experiments that should the stone be placed on red charcoal the first colour to fade would be the blue, allowing the red to become stronger and purer. As a matter of fact that is exactly what happened and the stone becoming a beautiful shade of red found its value multiplied tenfold. This improvement of the colour is quite a legitimate process, and the shade thus obtained will never change again.

But, of course, should a dye be used to colour a stone, thus *adding* to it, it would become a punishable offence. This was part of a verdict rendered about 20 years ago, by the Paris Chamber of Commerce of Pearl merchants. The verdict said clearly "that you may take away something from a stone. but you may not add to it."

Of course, it was argued at the time that this was not quite clear enough, for any dishonest lapidary could, for instance, cut out one carat from a stone, then add to it $\frac{3}{4}$ carat of some colour ing chemical or agent, and try to prove by the weight of the stone that it had lost and not gained . . .

This verdict, of course, referred to pearls that can be peeled like an onion, skin after skin, so as to obtain the most interesting . . . and costly colour, and that, in dishonest hands, could also be dyed.

CHAPTER IV

MINING IN CEYLON

MINING for gems, or gemming, is practised here in a most independent and primitive manner. It is done by individuals or very small groups of villagers, land-owners, paddy cultivators on planters' estates and by occasional lessees of a piece of Crown land. In that case the labourers set to clear and cultivate the land, add a little gemming to their other activities. Most of it is done in the Ratnapura district, and in the villages surrounding the " City of gems " as it is called in Sinhalese.

Most gems are obtained from alluvial deposits. They are not usually found in the lower reaches of large rivers, but in those of smaller volume in the upper reaches of valleys in mountainous districts. This is because of the sorting action effected by running water, according to the specific gravity of the transported material, the heavier stones being left near their source, in the mother rock. On this account alluvial mining can only be carried out by small gangs of coolies, using very primitive tools and methods.

In the stream itself, working only requires one tool : the prospector's pan. It is a shallow circular dish, one to two feet in diameter and with sides sloping gradually to the bottom, like a slice cut from a sphere. It is of metal generally, but sometimes it may be of wood or woven fibres, like a flat basket. The gem-washer, standing in the stream coops up gravel from the bottom, with his (or her) pan. The pan, while still under water, is given a circular up and down motion, being at the same time slightly tilted. The finer dirt and particles fall out over the edge and the heavy mineral, gold included, works its way to the bottom of the pan, beneath the lighter pebbles. This operation can be expedited with the hand. Sometimes the whole panful is turned upside down on the ground, where the gems can be picked out of the top, or sorted out with a quick eye.

Gem bearing gravel dug from shallow pits on the bank of the stream, is carried down to the stream and treated in the same manner.

The pits dug in alluvial deposits or in paddy fields, cannot be called mines. In Ceylon they are always small pits, only a few dozen feet deep. Some have no more than a depth of ten feet. The arrangements for holding up their sides and bailing out the water are still very primitive. I think they were worked in the same way centuries ago. They are not much more advanced in the ruby mines of Mogok, in Burmah. Only occasionally have small improvements been made by a gemmer. The villagers here would certainly feel embarrassed if they were to be asked to use " modern " tools to hasten or improve the work. They do not want to be hastened and are suspicious of improvements. What their fathers did and the way they did it, is good enough for them, as long as it was good enough for their ancestors. Yet who can blame them for not being afflicted with the modern love of speed or the desire to get rich quick ?

Years ago I remember asking my servant boy to do something and adding " Quickly." He replied, " Yes master, but not quickly." You see, that is the happy spirit ! If you are in a hurry don't come to the East. " Not quickly " has since become one of the charms of this country and one of my reasons for my great love of it. While the capital of the gemming industry is Ratnapura, about 70 miles south-east from Colombo, the main districts are all round this town, the most important villages being Eheliagoda, Balangoda and Rakwana. That does not mean that the best thing for you to do, if you are a serious buyer of various gems is to proceed directly there as soon as you reach Ceylon.

For you may be very disappointed and find nothing in Ratnapura, or at least not the choice of stones you imagined might be found there. Uncut stones are regularly sold by auction in Ratnapura, in lots that may amount from 20 to 100,000 rupees.

It has been many times my experience that any fine gem found in Ratnapura was almost immediately sent to Colombo where the head office of the " miners " is often established. In any case Colombo remains the trading centre.

Most amazingly some of the pits are sterile or barren of anything but gravel, pebbles and a flow of muddy water. When such a pit has been opened it will be refilled and another dug a few feet further. In this new pit—as an astonishing contrast and as if by magic—you may find at a depth of eight or ten feet a most extraordinary assortment of different gems, of various chemical origins and crystallized, by nature, in totally different systems. That is how at the same lucky spot, many kinds of stones can be found, in the same clay, sand and gravel. Not only blue sapphires, of twenty assorted tints, but corundums of every colour, white, yellow, pink, purple, etc., together with chrsyo-beryls, cats' eyes, spinels of all shades, tourmalines of all colours and many varieties of quartz, all on the same gem-bearing land. The cavern of Ali-Baba was nothing compared to this abundance. After having hoarded this treasure thousands of years, Nature at last gives it up. It even happens that Nature overly generous lets you find in that same pit a piece of pure gold which will make the setting for the stone of your choice.

I have been offered once or twice the lease of a plot of land near Ratnapura, where I could do some gemming and try my luck. I never believed in getting something for nothing and my reply has always been the same : " You make the pit yourself and when you find a good stone I shall always be happy to buy it at a good price." Another reason I never gave, is that I refuse to endanger my health by sleeping on a camp bed besides the pit, so as to see that no one robs me. I am subject to colds !

It is so easy for a cooly digging inside the pit, during the day, to stick one or two pieces in the mud walls, when, with a rapid glance, he has detected a good colour in a stone just found. At dead of night he intends to come and retrieve it.

Here I cannot resist the desire to tell you a genuine story about gemming, by an outsider, having no connection with gem traders. In fact he called himself a doctor, (of gems) ? He had a small piece of land and wanted to sell it at a higher figure than it was worth, so he secretly buried some rough stones a few feet below the surface and brought to the spot, in great mystery, on a moonless night, three prospective buyers carrying spades.

Arriving at the " slated " spot, he said, " Dig here." Under the pale light of their storm lantern they soon found eight or ten rough stones. (They had been buried close to each other for convenience's sake). The hole was quickly filled up and the " rich strike " placed in a small box. On examination of their find the next day, they were all very satisfied and their hopes of a rapidly made fortune was visible in their greedy eyes. One only of these stones puzzled them and they came to me for my opinion. It was a pale sky blue stone of about 80 carats. Its shape was a cone with six irregular sides, but they were not smooth as they should have been. Villagers call it " The Devil's cut " because these are the six natural facets Nature has given the rough crystallised corundum. These facets were coarse and showed very visible traces of rubbing against hard and rough surfaces. On seeing this, I remembered vividly that I had often seen the " doctor " rub something against a stone wall at certain street corners in Colombo, and the " thing " always disappeared in his pocket as soon as he saw me approaching. It was, of course, a small lump of pale coloured glass, which he had rubbed to the shape of an irregular hexagonal pyramid, very clumsily indeed . . .

As I had been consulted in my professional capacity, I felt it my painful duty to declare that " specimen " a valueless imitation.

The " doctor " on hearing this, poured upon me a wealth of epithets and insults such that, even today, I can still hear them. If words could kill I would have been well and truly dead. His defence was attack. The flower of his rhetoric came when he snatched the " gem " from my hand and slobbered " You people come to our country to cheat us of our valuable stones, by pronouncing them imitations, in order to buy them for a few rupees."

I don't think he sold his " gem land " after that . . .

CHAPTER V

WHAT IS A CARAT?

CENTURIES ago, gems were weighed with grains of barley, wheat or rice and in some countries with the seeds peculiar to the region.

In India it was a small bright red seed with a little black cap at one end called Rati. Gems are still sold by the Rati, which is less than our carat. (Of course, when Indians buy gems they demand the carat . . .). Of all the seeds in use, preference was given to a Brazilian one : the Karaat. This one was selected with very good reason. Each one of these seeds, whether large or small have the same weight.

The Karaat was also subdivided in four grains. Until the first world war, our modern carat, adapted from that Brazilian bead was still mentioned as four grains for one carat diamond or two grains, for half a carat, although the official subdivisions of our carat were counted by ½, ¼, 1/8, 1/16, 1/32 and 1/64th. These subdivisions were found very difficult to cope with, and therefore after 1920, the carat became the metric carat with decimal subdivisions, so that now ¼ carat is one twenty-fifth and ½ is one fiftieth of a carat. This new metric carat had to be reduced by 2½ per cent. to make it metric. So that now, instead of 100 carats as of old, you get only 97½ carats with the new metric weight, stamped on each of the weights C.M. (carat metrique). Five carats, now, weigh exactly one gramme, (or about 3 grains in English measure).

Beads and Coins for Weight

In Ceylon only gold is weighed with a local red bead called Manjary. Twelve of these beads are also called by local goldsmiths, a Pagoda. Twenty-eight manjaries make the weight of one gold sovereign, or about 8 grammes. Sometimes, they use

70 cents of Ceylon silver coins to equal the weight of one gold sovereign.

One 25 cents silver coin ..	..	..	10 manjaries
One 25 cents silver coin ..	..	..	10 manjaries
One 10 cents silver coin ..	..	..	4 manjaries
One 10 cents silver coin ..	..	..	4 manjaries
70 cents	Total	..	28 manjaries

or 8 grammes—1 gold sovereign.

These silver coins are now out of circulation and no longer legal tender in Ceylon, but all jewellers and all goldsmiths have kept a few of them for the purpose of weighing gold, when buying or selling. Some of the beads are kept for subdivisions of the 10 cents —at least 3 of them otherwise the 10 cents coin would have to be in 4 quarters like a miniature tart.

Here again these vegeta weights are used regularly for the same reason than the Brazilian Karaat, because each one whether big or small weighs exactly the same.

The public is nearly always at a loss to understand the difference between say 18 carat gold or a gem of 18 carats weight.

What is a carat ? I am often asked. Is it a weight or a measure ? As a matter of fact it is both, and this is how and when.

You already know that the carat is a weight for precious stones and prices are always calculated per carat. For gold it is a comparison of purity based upon the weight in carats. This is how : Pure powder or nugget gold as found in the mines is called 24 carats. If 24 carat weight of that powder is mixed with 2/24th of alloy you get 2/24th more gold but you have reduced its purity to 22 carats. If you mix 6/24ths alloy you get 18 carats If you mix 24 carat weight of alloy you will have doubled your lump of gold which will now weigh 48 carats, but you will have reduced the purity of the metal by half, obtaining thus only 12 carats, And so on. . . .

CHAPTER VI

IN the earliest antiquity, gems were a symbol of authority. the Great Priest of the Temple of King Solomon had a breast-plate described in the Old Testament, with one large gem in the centre, surrounded by 12 others. They represented the 13 tribes of Israel. The ring of Solomon was the ring worn by his father, King David. One of the Pharaohs wore a gold ring in the shape of a key, which fitted the lock of the sarcophagus, in which, he would lay, mummified, at his death, wearing a necklace of scarabs carved of the gold speckled blue lapis-lazuli.

Very often in urgent cases, throughout history, Kings and Queens have entrusted their ring of authority to messengers sent on secret missions.

Oriental potentates have always given preference to the sealing of documents with their rings, rather than signing them. In many cases it saved them the trouble to learn how to write or to have to admit that they were illiterate.

Cleopatra drank pearls, a costly habit, which is in itself the best proof of her crass ignorance. Had she known that 88 per cent. of the pearl is calcium carbonate, she could have bought several ounces of it at the chemist shop on the corner, for the equivalent of a rupee, in Egyptian money, instead of impoverishing her " fellahs " by plundering the State Treasury for her costly cocktails.

Pearls of small size, called seed-pearls are found in the North-West of Ceylon and many Indian Rajahs drink these too. It certainly reminds them of Cleopatra, which is very romantic.

Nero liked to look through a large flat emerald, when, in the Amphitheatre, he enjoyed the sight of red Christian blood flowing on the yellow sand. May be the sight of it was even more exciting seen through the green screen of his unique " monocle."

In the days of Queen Elizabeth, (when diamond cutting had not yet been invented by the Flemish lapidary Ludowyk van Bercken) the Queen gave Sir Walter Raleigh a gold ring set with a rough pyramidal diamond with eight facets. On a day of spleen, while waiting for a royal audience, he wrote with the point of that diamond on one of the window panes of her antechamber. " Fain would I climb, but that I fear to fall."

Later when the Queen read this line, she completed the verse by engraving with her own diamond : " If thy heart fail thee do not climb at all."

Lucrezia Borgia and her family of. murderers—including a Pope—had certainly improved on the gentle art of murder. They would offer their friends a gold ring with a tiny secret compartment, below the gem, containing a violent poison that would slowly filtrate through the pores of the skin of the finger.

Catherine de Medicis improved on that with a microscopic needle, inside the shank, which scratched the finger so slightly, when the ring was slipped on, that nothing was felt by the victim and no trace of the scratch could even be seen, so tiny was it.

No doubt people in those wicked days must have regarded presents of jewellery with some suspicion.

Most certainly it must have given birth to such ridiculous beliefs, still persisting, that some gems bring bad luck.

To conclude these few remarks on peculiarities concerning gems, I wish to tell a very true little story.

Some years ago the lady dowager of an aristocratic family in Belgium, died suddenly, leaving an unsettled estate to her two grown up sons.

Among other things, she left jewellery that had been insured for years for £ 5,000. There was an assortment of rings, bracelets and brooches worth about half that amount, and a pearl necklace of fine Persian Gulf pink pearls valued at the other half.

The whole lot was brought up to me for a detailed valuation of each separate item, as the inheritance had to be equally divided between the two sons.

After proper examination of the jewels I called on the younger son. He was well known to me, as we had been at school together in Brussels and Antwerp. I was rather embarrassed, as I had found the pearl necklace to be an imitation, and I feared some past tragedy had been the cause of the exchange. My friend felt my embarrassment and asked smilingly.

"What is it ?"

"Your mother's pearl necklace was insured, was it not ?"

"Yes, for £2,500. Why ?"

"Are you quite sure it is this one ?"

"Positively. There is no other. I have known the slight defects on each one of the pearls for years."

"Don't you know," I asked, "that a pearl can be faithfully imitated in its shape, colour and defects, in fact exactly duplicated ? Many pearl necklaces of great value have been so copied and worn while the owners were travelling and when the genuine one was left in the bank ?"

My friend's face became very serious and a veil of sadness spread over his eyes.

"We have just discovered the secret of my mother's life . . . She married a very hard man, who made her life a long misery. And so she took a lover. He also belonged to our class, the son of another aristocratic family. Being young and reckless he gambled and fell into debt. In his last letter to my mother he spoke of disgrace, bankruptcy and suicide. I found the letter and that is how I know. Sometime later his debts were paid and he disappeared. My mother must have sold her necklace, paid his debts and all these years worn the imitation."

"How can I make the valuation and keep this a secret?"

"Very simply," he said. "I will let my brother take all the other jewels for his share, and I shall keep the pearl necklace . . . and the secret."

"It is a costly sacrifice you are making."

"I have two very strong reasons for doing so: my mother's honour . . ."

"And the other?"

"The other man was my father . . ."

CHAPTER VII

EMERALDS are not found in Ceylon, but I could not write about gems without speaking of this stone of great beauty for two important reasons :

(1) Because the emerald is a beryl, in fact the beryl queen. But, in spite of the fact that some Beryls are found in Ceylon, the emerald is not.

(2) Because the emerald is the most valuable and the most costly of all precious stones. This fact is always surprising to the public who think that diamonds come first.

That is wrong ; so wrong that they do not even come second. Before them we have the ruby a royally proud gem indeed. It is only after these two that comes the bright and invulnerable diamond.

But that does not mean that there are no cheap emeralds and rubies. There are plenty of them, whose colour and quality poor.

To command the highest price, the emerald must be of the right shade, and that is the colour of the French liqueur called " Creme de Menthe." Such a gem, if at least five carats in size, with perfection of shape and lustre and almost spotless, may cost as much as 4,000 to 5,000 rupees per carat or more.

I said " almost spotless " because there is no such emerald of that size absolutely pure under the magnifying glass. It is in the nature of that stone to have visible small flaws, on account of microscopic pockets filled with gas or liquid, or to be specked with dots and traces of visible crystallisation, due to the pressure of rocks.

These are so natural to the emerald that many people regard a stone with suspicion if it does not show any so natural flaws. This also accounts for the fact that if other stones can be imitated with more or less skill, the emerald has not yet been faithfully reproduced, except as doublet in which the top part, the table, is real emerald of poor colour, soldered upon another such piece, and a very thin film of grass green enamel slipped in between table and cullet and "soldered" together. In fact this so-called doublet should be called triplet. They are made in Paris, for local use, and sold as the nearest reproduction of the emerald with genuine beryl pieces. Some emeralds have been synthetically made, lately, by recrystallizing the same chemical ingredients. (Chattam emeralds, California).

Doublets are really a masterpiece of the lapidary art and cost only about Rs. 20 to Rs. 30 per carat, a low figure indeed for such a beautiful—almost genuine stone. I have seen before this war, wonderful specimens of "soldered emeralds" cut by friends in Paris, that even experienced jewellers could not identify as such, with the naked eye, but only with a special colour screen which shows real emeralds in a bluish shade. The doublets, of course, could not show the usual blue of real emeralds, when seen with that instrument, as the green colouring of doublets is an artificial colour, although the whole gem is made up with two real pieces of beryl, with their natural flaws and gas pockets. Flawless doublets cost less than doublets made with the usual defects of real emeralds, which is an emphatic proof that flaws identify at a glance an emerald as genuine. The finest emeralds were found in India, but since the last century the Golconda mines are abandoned or bare of any gems. They were the finest in the world, some of them commanding as much as Rs. 10,000 per carat. They are all hoarded in large quantities in the coffers of Indian Rajahs. Unfortunately they are all of a hopeless cut or shape. Some are even polished like large beads with a hole pierced for use in necklaces, and therefore they have no commercial value on modern markets, unless they are skilfully recut. But that would cost a loss in weight of at least 50 to 60 per cent. Huge cabochons emeralds are also embedded in thrones, swords, jewellery boxes, idols, etc., but these are enhanced in colour by the slipping, underneath the stone, of coloured tinfoil that gives it that deceptive shade.

Nowadays emeralds come from the Ural mountains, Russia, in poor and medium blackish green quality and the best from Columbia, in South America. There are also some in Brazil, another country rich in gems, like Ceylon. Another peculiar thing about that stone is that Madagascar has even more specimens of different beryls than Ceylon, but still no emeralds, queen of the Beryl family.

The second best to the emerald as I have already said is the ruby, provided of course, it has the perfect red colour which for rubies is called pigeon blood.

Ceylon, of course, is well known for its rubies and has a full range of colours from the sweet baby rose, through a ladder of at least twenty deepening shades, up to sometimes, the real pigeon blood, but this perfect shade is rarely found here. Burma is the cradle of this gem, but do not complain when exhorbitant prices are asked for it. Ceylon rubies are paler and cheaper. Those I refer to as being worth more than diamonds come from Mogok in Burma. These crystallizations are of small sizes usually embedded in the mother rock. Whereas in Ceylon they are found in separate hexagonal crystals of fairly large sizes. Therefore the Burma product is much smaller. These pigeon blood stones weigh usually, when cut and polished, only one, two or three carats. A perfect ruby is rarely as heavy as four carats, and one can count on the fingers of one hand how many of these rubies weighing five carats that are to be found in the world's market. The mineral colouring matter in the Burma gem pits is much richer than in Ceylon, and so, Ceylon rubies, paler in colour cost very much less than the Mogok type. The Ceylon ruby costs from 30 to 50 or even 100 rupees per carat for the rose ones, 100 to 200 for a deeper pink and from 300 to 600 rupees per carat, and more, for fine red specimens. But if they have the pigeon blood shade, prices may go from 1,000 to 4,000 rupees a carat, if they are also large and perfectly pure. It is by comparing the colours that you can follow the rise, up the ladder of shades, because a colour that you think perfect, will soon reveal it is nothing of the kind when compared with other colours.

This of course applies to all gems: they must be compared and your eye will be able to see better and better. It may amuse you to know that very striking colour effects appear when rubies are exposed to ultra-violet rays. Either in crystal form or as cut stones, rubies are seen to glow with a brilliant red light, as if they were on fire. They, then, fully justify the names given to them by the Greeks and Romans: anthrax (anthracite) and carbunculus which both mean a glowing coal. (Although carbuncle is, in reality, a red carbochon garnet). When removed from the influence of the violet rays, the red colour shown by the stone itself is very poor in comparison. Ladies who wish to display their rubies to the most striking advantage should move under such a light. Then the rubies would look as if they had caught fire and were burning, but the lady herself would become invisible. Were she wearing a white dress it would show a beautiful bluish colour, but above the dress no face at all, except a few black spots, revealing her false teeth, that her lover once compared to pearls. . . .

To come now to the third most valuable gem, the diamond, I will reserve for it another chapter, well deserved by such an important subject in the next edition.

Before closing this chapter, I would like you to enjoy a "bon mot" I heard a few days ago about precious stones.

I went to see "The Snake Pit." In a lunatic asylum, two women are talking and one of them—sophisticated type of the last century—confides to her companion:

"I have the Hope diamond."

To which the other one replies:

"I have the Hopeless emerald. . . ."

WHAT PRECIOUS STONES ARE MADE OF

IT is not the object of this study to be scientific or technical but I want my readers to understand a little about the minerals and chemicals that compose gems. I will make this as short as possible.

Until chemistry came into its own, early in the 19th century, it was not possible to name and describe gems correctly. Gems are composed of chemical elements just as drugs, poisons and generally all the contents of a druggist's shop. Their true nature depends primarily upon their chemical composition. Even a slight knowledge of chemistry is very useful for a proper appreciation of the different kinds of gems, but if one wants to know their actual composition the aid of a skilled analytical chemist is needed. I do not intend to go as far as that, but I will try to express a few fundamentals in the next page or so.

Ninety-two different kinds of basic substances are known to chemists.

These are the chemical elements which, either alone, or in combination with one another, make up all the different kinds of matter known to us. For example, metal aluminium and oxygen gas are chemical elements known to all of us. The combination of these two by burning aluminium in oxygen gives a white powder of aluminium oxide, called alumina. When this is crystallized it becomes the mineral corundum. When this corundum is dyed with small amounts of colouring matter, we have the sapphire, if blue or the ruby if red. This is, of course, the work of nature and not the laboratory.

Neither aluminium nor oxygen can be split up, but ruby or sapphire can be split up into aluminium and oxygen. This, however would not be an economical way of manufacturing aluminium pots and pans or of producing cylinders of oxygen. By using the exact proportions 27 tons of aluminium and 24 tons of oxygen the result will be 51 tons of ruby or sapphire and conversely from 51 tons of ruby or sapphire there could be manufactured 27 tons of pots and pans . . . regardless of the extraordinarily excessive cost. This is to emphasize the fact that gems are only a compound of various minerals well known to us. The only exception is the diamond which consists of a single element : carbon. All the other gems, regardless of their contents of various minerals, all contain oxygen.

Of the ninety-two basic substances, twenty-six are found in the composition of gems. Of course, these twenty-six, when combined in different ways, form several compounds of an endless variety. Some gems, like tourmalines, contain twelve different elements and about fifty shades.

A scientific classification must be based on their chemical composition since, on this, together with their crystalline composition, all their other characters depend. Any other classifications based on colour, importance or rarity are quite arbitrary.

It is of some interest and importance to know what the various gems are composed of, but as a rule, this knowledge cannot be applied where stones are concerned, for chemical tests involve the complete destruction of the material and are therefore of no practical use to us. For instance, a chemical test for diamonds would mean the burning of the material and collecting the resulting carbon dioxide. We must, therefore, depend or rely upon a physical test for purposes of determination. If, however, we should meet an entirely new kind of gem, of which rough material is available, a complete analysis must, of course, be made for a thorough investigation by mineralogical methods.

Testing Gems

The only test I can advise you to make, when in doubt about the genuineness of a stone is by ascertaining its specific gravity and its hardness.

In order to test accurately the specific gravity there is a series of different liquids in which gems either float or sink, half way or right to the bottom.

As for hardness one can buy easily a collection of rough stones, gems of course, by which a softer stone can be scratched with a harder one, the reverse process not being feasible, as I have explained in another chapter of this book.

Of course, the best test is the examination of the false gem with a strong magnifying glass which will show the defects, even minute ones, to be of a different structure than caused by a natural crystallization and the betraying bubbles of air. As for myself as soon as I set eyes on a stone, I know if it is real or false by the colour. If we agree that there are, for instance, twenty different shades of blue in a sapphire, I know at once if the particular shade is real or false because I have not yet seen a single imitation that had the right colour, whatever its shade. Not once have I found a colour perfectly reproduced. That is, of course, with my own eyes, and that may not apply to many others.

Another of my own tests is touching the gem without looking at it. I take it between my two first fingers and slightly squeeze the stone, with a dry gesture of the fingers. First, I feel the natural coolness, characteristic of a good gem and second, according to the type of gem, I get an astringent feeling or a slippery touch. Of course, this "touch" system is the result of long experience and I can give no easy explanation for it. It has taken me thirty years to learn this, apart from the knowledge acquired and inherited from my family, that have been gem dealers for several generations.

Reconstructed Gems

Just over a quarter of a century ago, a French chemist found a process for imitating very accurately sapphires and rubies. His name was Verneuil and his process, is the closest to Nature's own work. The gems thus obtained were called scientific sapphires and reconstructed rubies. They all contained the same chemicals provided by nature, with colour added, of course, but they could easily be detected as the stones were visibly streaked with curved lines or portions of a circle. They had almost the same colour, almost the same hardness, almost the same specific gravity, but none had the structure or qualities of the genuine stone. If touched with a drop of water, that drop, instead of contracting narrowly and remaining on the stone, would spread, flat, as it does upon any sheet of glass. They were sold at the time for what they were, at a few rupees per carat with no attempt at deception and, of course, not to the type of people who are interested in buying real gems. Some dishonest people, outside the gem trade, played upon the credulity of their friends or acquaintances, but no established jeweller ever tried to sell them as genuine. Since then, this process has been enormously improved upon, and today it needs a very careful examination to see the difference. The weight is very near to perfection and so are the hardness and colour. The drop of water holds tightly and there are no more curved lines visible. But an ordinary colour screen or crystallograph will show that it is only a very perfect imitation, that no gem dealer would ever think of including in his trade. Unless, of course, he advertises the fact that he sells imitations, when he does so at an adequate figure, and openly.

SUPERSTITIONS

THERE are superstitions of all kinds: some people never have a haircut on Friday, avoid thirteen, hate meeting a cripple or a female hunchback. Some will not be the third to take a light from the same match, or will refuse to pass under a ladder. All these things are supposed to bring bad luck. Does it matter much whether it is true or not as long as one believes in it ? To be honest, I must admit that I believe in some of them. Don't you ? Why ? There are, of course, explanations, but that is not the point I wish to make here and now. On the other hand, there are also some more or less foolish beliefs about what is supposed to bring good luck.

All these superstitions are as old as the world itself, and no proof of an undeveloped mind. In every civilised society this nonsense goes on, without shame or excuse. A few coincidences have maintained them through several centuries and given the impression of a mystic or occult power, beyond our control. We have reached the point where we accept them as truly unavoidable ills, and we dare not discuss them. That, of course, explains why they have come to stay. Some are so very striking that even science gave up trying any explanation. Some have come to us from black continents or from savages and have become part of our daily tergiversations and struggles.

Take, for instance, this most mysterious and cruel belief of the aborigines of Australia and New Zealand that should a bone be pointed at you, you will die of a slow and sure death. It seems absurd, but it has happened innumerable times and no one can explain why.

Opals

The opal, that most fascinating of all gems, full of magic and sometimes of a beauty that is awe-inspiring, is very often the result of petrified wood or fossilized animal bones, the transformation having taken place million of years ago in Australia the country where they fear threats with a bone. Is that one of the reasons why—most unjustly, I must say—this splendid gem is accused of bringing bad luck to anyone not born in October? Who knows? If you want my personal and somewhat cynical opinion, I think that this unfair accusation has been the result of improper competition amongst importers of the stone.

In 1870, when the rocks of White Cliffs and Lightning Ridge were discovered in the heart of the Australian bush, it was so difficult to travel and reach the beds and layers of these sandy rocks, that opals, although plentiful and cheap, in that country were, yet, rather rare in Europe, and very few jewellers were able to obtain any. Because of their novelty, the demand must have been great and there was a flourishing trade, the result of their sudden appearance on the market. I can easily imagine that the jewellers who had none in stock must have told their clients not to buy these stones as they brought bad luck, in order to stop their sale.

I have been given another additional reason for that difficulty in buying them at the mines. As it has to do with the very unusual and original way of acquiring them at the pits in Australia, I think it will prove of interest to my readers. Apparently the currency preferred by the diggers of opals is cases of Scotch whisky that have to be carried across the bush in covered wagons, no easy task in a country where roads are practically non-existent.

Another paradox is that people who point at the opal and mention it as a bringer of bad luck are usually those who buy them, as if to defy destiny. Ceylon has no opals, but imports them in large quantities, in their rough form. They are cut in Galle, for the Colombo jewellers' passenger trade and they are sold at 2, 4, 8 and even 10 rupees per carat. This price is, of course, for the cut and polished stones. These operations are done by hand, with great skill, at a much cheaper rate than in Australia so, paradoxically, opals are, as a rule, sold in Ceylon for a lower price than in the country of their origin.

Other opals are found in Bohemia, the milky kind, and a multi-coloured transparent gem in Mexico, which has a somewhat jellied appearance, such as it was in fact before it solidified in the mother rock. A curious fact is that all their rainbow-like multitude of colours becomes invisible if the stone is seen by transparence. This, of course, is the wrong way to look at them, as all you see is several cracks and no colour, or at least what appears as cracks to you, for if they were really so, the stone would fall in pieces. Another peculiarity of this gem is that the colours one admires so much are produced by contents of water that mixed itself in it when it got solidified, millions of years ago. Consisting of silica with a variable amount of water—three to seven per cent.—or of dried silica jelly, the opal is one of the very few stones who has no crystallization at all and which has not yet yielded to attempts to reproduce it in imitation stones.

The opals that show all their colours upon a deep and dark ground are called black opals or precious opals although they are dark brown, green or blue, but not milky as the other kinds are. The usual fire opal is worth from Rs. 5 to Rs. 20 per carat, while the black opal may cost up to Rs. 100 per carat. One also finds some wavy yellow opals absolutely colourless and semi-transparent —containing no water, of course—but these, if offered for sale, cut and polished, have no value at all.

Moonstones

Let us now be more cheerful and speak of at least one gem—from Ceylon—that is said to bring Good luck : the moonstone.

I know of no other stone that is popularly believed to bring good luck and that stone is almost exclusive to Ceylon.

There are some yellow specimens found in Madagascar or some brownish felspar found in Switzerland, but only in Ceylon can you find the clear white species with a ravishing bluish glint or sheen, moving freely in the gem like moonshine upon a lake. Small flakes or flat chips are common enough and are used in cheap silver jewellery, sold for a few rupees. But don't jump to the conclusion that moonstones are of little value or worthless. There are beautiful specimens cut in the shape of a cabochon, weighing 15 to 25 carats, absolutely pure and very blue in their reflections. Such pieces are really gems of value and rather rare. If the white shining large pieces are worth from Rs. 2 to Rs. 4 per carat, there are those blue ones that may cost from 5 to 10 rupees per carat and they are sometimes very difficult to obtain. If you wear a ring with a cabochon moonstone in a theatre or in a ball room, the numerous lights around you will all be reflected in the gem and give birth to living and luminous moving points.

Large pieces of gem quality are in constant demand from all over the world, but Ceylon cannot supply the tremendous orders received. It is, of course, left to the art of the lapidary, when polishing them, to bring the sheen or luminous glitter they contain, to the centre, at the bottom of the cabochon, so that the moonstone may reflect the maximum lustre and brilliancy. Some have only a thin and narrow silk in them and here again the cutter can give the stone the appearance of a cat's eye which is fancifully called cat's eye-moonstone. Ceylon cutters, I must say are very clever in exploiting all the qualities of a rough gem and bring them out to advantage.

Gem-cutting

This, in spite of old-fashioned ways and primitive tools. The cutter sits on the ground in front of a wooden axle three feet long, on the left side of which a metal disc is fixed, revolving with the motions of the axle. In his right hand the cutter holds a stick with a rope, shaped like a bow and that rope is turned once around the axle enclosing it in a kind of loop. With rhythmic movements forward and backwards he gives this primitive contraption a rotative impulse of about three turns to the left, three turns to the right. The disc fixed on the left side turns, of course, with it. It is upon that disc that he holds the gem with his left hand and grinds the facets of the stone one by one in their geometrical design. The stone, if small or of medium size is embedded in a solid compound of cement or shellac and if large enough is held with the fingers. For every facet he must take the stone out of that solid mass and re-embed it to grind the next facet. Sometimes he has to do this sixty or eighty times, till the stone is completely cut and polished.

According to the hardness of the stone that disc is either of steel, cast iron, copper, wood or even felt and must be smeared with various ingredients. On the principle that "diamond cuts diamond" every gem is cut with the help of different powders or oils.

For the cutting of gems of the corundum family, the hardest of all, such as rubies or sapphires, emery of different fineness is successively used, and that is black sapphire or carborundum in the form of wheels or powder. A softer abrasive would not cut the gem and a harder one such as bort or diamond powder, would scratch or break a sapphire. I must here emphasize the fact that the hardness of gems as classified in Mohs's Scale is very relative, and huge differences may be found between two successive numbers.

For instance, if corundum is nine and diamond ten it does not mean that diamond is ten per cent. harder than sapphire. It is, in fact, over a hundred times harder and several hundred times harder than quartz, seven on the scale. This has been proved by grinding tests, the best, naturally. And we get then scratchings on a stone by another that cannot, itself, be scratched. Since the ring of St. Peter, Bishops and Princes of the Holy Church have always worn a large gem, usually an amethyst set upon a broad shank, this because it is worn over the gloved finger. This Episcopal ring is the mark of temporal authority. Few are those who know, when they kiss the Bishop's hand that it is upon the stone itself they should place their lips.

Bishops very often wear a gold chain with a gem-studded cross (usually red garnets) but that cross if awe-inspiring is not specially a mark of their high office. Don't forget that wedding rings are also a symbol of authority !

With all due respect for anything referring to Church dignitaries, I would like to tell you another little true story on the subject of these rings.

In 1932, three Chinese and four French priests from dioceses in China went to Rome and were ordained Bishops by the Holy Father himself.

The three Chinese received their Episcopal rings from the Pope's hand and they showed them to me, in Colombo, when the French boat " Aramis " passed through on its way to Shanghai.

They were three beautiful Ceylon amethysts, all oval in shape, weighing about 20 carats each and set in magnificent embossed gold rings, carved on each side of the stone with small winged angels' heads as those painted by Raphael.

These amethysts were undoubtedly gemmed in Ceylon, because they were of that most perfect and unadulterated colour of purple, we usually call " Bishop's purple." It is only in Ceylon that this colour is found absolutely clear and pure.

Amethysts from Brazil have a tinge of brown blended in the purple, that gives them the wrong shade.

The four Frenchmen had no rings yet and they asked me if I could make some for them. By a curious coincidence, I was leaving for Saigon in the same ship and I promised to make the four rings for them during the trip. I still remember how very surprised they were by this statement of mine. I smiled and asked them to select the stones then and there, promising to deliver the amethysts duly set before we reached Saigon.

I am not under obligation to tell my clients how I do things, provided I keep my promises to them, but I must confess all to my readers, who have a right to know.

Surprising things always appear very simple once they have been explained, don't they ?

Well I knew we were to have a whole day ashore in Penang as well as in Singapore.

I took the four gems with me, sufficient gold to set them with and had them half made in Penang and finished in Singapore, for I knew a Sinhalese workshop in both these towns. The evening we left Singapore Harbour, I was ready to supply the four Episcopal rings to my Bishops. They were very surprised indeed, when on deck, where we were then standing, I gave to each his " emblem of authority."

VARIETIES OF GEMS FOUND IN CEYLON

Corundum.—Blue Sapphire, Star Sapphire, Ruby, Star Ruby, King Sapphire, white, yellow, pink, purple and greenish sapphire.

Hardness : 9. *Specific Gravity :* 4 ·0.

Beryls—Lilac, pink, red, called Morganite ; Blue : aqua-marine. Golden yellow Heliodor, Green : emerald. These last two are not found in Ceylon.

Hardness : 7½. *Specific Gravity :* 2 ·67.

Chrysoberyls.—Yellow, greenish yellow, brown, Cat's Eye. Greenish brown or olive, green in daylight and pinkish or red in artificial light : Alexandrite, a rare Ceylon gem.

Hardness : 8½. *Specific Gravity :* 3 ·70.

Spinels.—Blue, greenish, red, pink, purple, mauve and black. The latter, found only in Ceylon, is also called Ceylonite.

Hardness : 8. *Specific Gravity :* 3 ·7.

Tourmalines.—A very large range of brilliant colours, the most valued one being the green, in several different shades, but not the emerald green. A ladder of yellows, brown, rosewood, purple, lilac, chartreuse, and a bright deep golden shade. In Ceylon, tourmalines rarely have two distinctive colours in each half part of the stone, such as pink and apple green, as found in the Brazilian ones. Among semi-precious stones, fairly cheap in price, this is the most interesting gem.

Hardness : 7½. *Specific Gravity :* 3 ·0 to 3 ·2.

Garnets.—Red, wine, brown, chocolate. The green variety is not found in Ceylon.

Hardness : 7 to 7½. *Specific Gravity :* 3 ·0 to 3 ·2.

Cinnamon Stone.—Orange, brown, yellowish-red and bright tango. Of the garnet family.

Hardness : 7 to 7½. *Specific Gravity :* 3·0 to 3·2.

Amethyst.—Pale lilac, violet, purple, brownish-purple, lie de vin. Of the quartz family.

The perfect purple as worn by Bishops is found only in Ceylon.

Hardness : 7. *Specific Gravity :* 2·65.

Quartz.—A large assortment of browns, yellows, lemon, pale blues, greenish and pinkish-whites; white and orange. Some are considered Ceylon topazes, aqua-marine or water sapphire.

Hardness : 7. *Specific Gravity :* 2·65.

Zircons.—A few white and pale sea green ones are found in Ceylon. But many are found in their crude brown or greenish primitive colour, which can be changed or rather transmuted into bright shades by the electrical treatment given them, very skilfully in Siam, from where the "finished" gem is imported to Ceylon. Very often they are mistakenly mixed with tourmalines, among which they get chipped or scratched being notably softer. The Zircon is the brightest of all Ceylon gems.

Hardness : 7 to 7½. *Specific Gravity :* 4·0 to 4·7.

Moonstone.—A bright Felspar found almost exclusively in Ceylon. the best specimens are crystal white with a blue, moving sheen, comparable to moonlight. Second qualities are white, like Mother-of-pearl, and others are yellowish or brownish. White pieces, not suitable for making jewels are melted and used in large quantities for glazing the finest porcelain and art statuettes. This is the only stone said to bring luck.

Hardness : 6. *Specific Gravity :* 2·56.

Agathe, Onyx, Chalcedony and similar hard stones are found in a large assortment of colours. Suitable for beads and for signet rings that can be engraved with a sharp rough diamond.

Hardness : 6½. *Specific Gravity :* 2·6.

Pearls.—Seed pearls and slightly larger sizes are found in the pearl banks of the Gulf of Mannar and other places along the Ceylon coast. They are used by the dozen, in ornaments and jewellery very appreciated by Sinhalese ladies. Larger pearls, as used in pearl necklaces are rare. They are all natural pearls, such as found in the Persian Gulf. None are cultured.

Hardness : 3½. *Specific Gravity :* 2·7.

MOHS'S SCALE OF HARDNESS

1. Talcum
2. Gypsum
3. Calcite
4. Fluorite
5. Apatite
6. Felspar
7. Quartz
8. Topaz
9. Corundum
10. Diamond

A THOUSAND MILLION YEAR OLD GEM STONE DISCOVERED IN CEYLON. MAY BE A NEW MINERAL

BEFORE concluding this little booklet, I substantiate what I have stated, to the effect that Ceylon is one of the greatest gem-producing countries in the world, by reproducing an extract from an article that appeared in the London Gemmological Journal of April, 1954.

At the 1954 Gemmological Exhibition of Great Britain, " four members had responded to the invitation to ' exhibit.' Sir James Walton, the Vice-Chairman, Mr. B. W. Anderson, Mr. Keith Mitchell and Mr. F. Ullmann. And although not by design, the aspects of gemmology that were demonstrated by each of their collections were entirely different and illustrated its many sided appeal.

It might be said that the star stone shown by Mr. Mitchell was the " star " of the evening, for it appears fairly certain that it represents a mineral which in this form has not been discovered before. The stone came from Ceylon, having been cut because of its natural asterism and being sent to Mr. Mitchell by Mr. F. L. D. Ekanayake, a keen collector whose gemmological knowledge enabled him to recognise the interesting features of the gem. Of a greyish-green colour, the cabachon cut and polished stone was investigated at the Hatton Garden Laboratory where the first findings suggested that it was glass and because of the lead content noted, that it was artificial glass. As a result of this the stone was sent to the well known School of Glass Technology at Sheffield University for further examination. The University confirmed that the constants found were correct but they further discovered the presence of thorium as a major constituent and that the stone was rather strongly radio-active.

It seems certain that this lead content is an end-product of the disintegration of the radio-active thorium and it is now considered that the stone is a natural mineral of the " metamict " type. Calculations based on its radio-activity suggest that this has been going on for a thousand million years."

Mr. F. L. D. Ekanayake is a Fellow of the Gemmological Institute of London and a keen collector of rare gem stones, with a good international reputation, he has been responsible for bringing to light very unusual and interesting gem stones and these are on record in the gemmological journals in London, but unfortunately he is not very well known in his own country, probably due to the fact that his hands are tied down as a Government Servant and is therefore unable to use his initiative and knowledge of gems in a wider sphere.

PEARL IMITATION

" And things are not what they seem."—*Longfellow*.

FOR the purpose of this little story, I shall call him Mr. Weissman. Of course he might have been Mr. Finkelstein, or Mr. Horowitz, but Weissman is good enough to describe a son of Israel, who had escaped with his life from the Ghetto and the Pogroms of Galicia, the country of his forefathers, for generations.

His father had grown tired of the yearly plundering in the Ghetto by drunken Russian soldiers and of thus contributing to the Pay of the Tsar's Imperial Guard.

So, he advised his son to emigrate to France, country always hospitable to refugees and political outcasts. A Yiddish nucleus colony was already settled there and he would do well to join it. He could do as others had done : open a Kosher delicatessen shop, a distillery of Shlibovitz, or start making coloured beads as he had seen them made in Gablonz.

Mr. Weissman, junior, being a poet at heart, chose a more romantic profession and decided to manufacture pearls.

He managed a display of his first attempt at the Paris International Exhibition of 1900, in the benevolent shadow of the newly built Eiffel Tower.

His necklaces became very popular and sold by the thousand, at six pence each. This left a fair percentage for him and for the seller as well, as they were simply made of porcelain beads, dipped in a sticky solution of collodion, fish scales reduced to a paste.

Of course it lost much of its beauty when once or twice the lady customer, having felt the weather, it had been soaked in acid perspiration. But still the white porcelain beads remained even when the sheen of the " pearl " had disappeared.

Or the lady could buy another necklace for six pence . . . and try to feel cooler.

Mr. Weissman made some quick money, but his success did not last. A better imitation had to be made and a new manufacturing process found.

The fact that the sheen and pearly lustre faded on a perspiring throat gave Mr. Weissman an idea, and his newly amassed wealth went into another commercial gamble. He decided that the pearly substance he used was good enough, but too vulnerable. Therefore he imagined that it would last much longer and yet retain its original beauty if he could enclose the collodion paste between two thin glass bulbs fitting inside each other. After several costly experiments, he produced the article he had imagined and it was beautiful. The only fault customers found with this new necklace was its too light weight and its fragility, as it could be crushed between two fingers. Often the tight embrace of two loving male arms was enough to cause the damage, and in Paris such embraces are rather frequent.

This new process, Mr. Weissman realised, was a good one, but he must make the "pearls" heavier, as near as possible to the specific gravity of real pearls.

After several trials and failures he found at last the proper process, used even today in making imitation pearls.

To advertise it in a rather spectacular way, he had a small gas stove placed in his shop window on which a bowl of boiling water bubbled all day, with one of his necklaces immerged in it. This was showmanship and salesmanship together.

He sold large quantities of his necklaces, first by the carat, then by the ounce and finally and definitely by the centimetre, regardless of the size of each pearl.

He sold them wholesale to shops, department stores and jewellers for ten shillings a necklace threaded with silk and fitted with a plated clasp. These in their turn added a shilling velvet box and sold the necklaces for one guinea each.

They all made good money including the box makers and the clasp manufacturers.

A few months later, imitation pearl necklaces appeared in various fashionable shops with a trade mark. There was the Zero Pearl, the Tic-Tac Pearl, the Birman Pearl.

Some sold at £3, £4 and £5, according to the rent paid by the various shops and the neighbourhood they were in. These were the only reasons for the difference in prices. Why ? Because these pearl necklaces were of only one same quality : all were bought at 10 shillings each and they were all made by Mr. Weissman.

At that time several people asked me which of these necklaces was the best, and I referred them all to the one and only manufacturer of only one standard quality :

"Ask Mr. Weissman, in Paris. . . ."

ELEPHANT HAIR JEWELS

SHORT and stocky, round faced and square shouldered, endowed with the joviality, humour and devil-may-care temperament of a habitual wine drinker—although sometimes he flared up as fast as boiling milk, (all Frenchmen do)—such was my old friend Antoine of Paris, a designer of costume jewellery. His creative mind was excellent and his taste faultless.

He was the very best type of the Parisian craftsman, one of the thousand small and independant manufacturers, working alone in their bedrooms, and supplying the trade with one or two different articles of art, thus adding to the large range of fine hand-made knick-knacks called " Articles de Paris."

Often a "creation " costing a few hundred francs only, makes a fine lady look like a million dollars.

He had started a gem business in his home town, Royat, a spa in Auvergne, where he had a smart shop, selling locally found amethysts and many coloured quartz. He made paper weights with large rough crystals, handles for silver powder boxes, chandeliers, blotters, rulers or inkstands with various kinds of malachite, jasper, carbuncles, agathe, calcedony, ortoclase, jet and amber. Few of these stones were of local origin, but that was not the funny part of his business.

Known as a " seaside lapidary," he encouraged his customers to go and collect pebbles from the mountains or the river beds, and bring them to him to be cut and polished. These pebbles were sometimes pretty enough, when wet, but mostly all of them were valueless. After a suitable interval of time, he would give his client a cheap stone of Brazilian origin, cut in Idar, Germany, and supplied to him, every year for the " season." The " valuable" pebble found by his proud client had, in the meantime been consigned to the rubbish heap.

Dishonesty ? A sense of humour ? Or was it that special kind of humour that enables you to laugh only when alone ?

In any case he had real amethysts beads, topaze beads and amber that were genuine and sold at their fair price. He had also imitation necklaces and these were sold as such. He advertised on his shop window " Genuine stones and imitations."

After the first world war he came to Paris and established the jewellery shop you can still see today at one of the corners of the rue Lafayette, the Hatton Garden of Paris. From there he started the fashion for jade and black onyx which spread the world over.

In 1923 as I was getting ready to come back to Ceylon, I paid him a friendly visit and asked him to show me his latest creations in fancy jewellery. Among several peculiar and very original articles of novelty jewellery, he showed me a range of strange jewels of every type made with a most novel material : the Elephant Hair.

For instance, a long brooch made out of five strands of elephant hair, representing the top of a music sheet with a gold " Clef de Sol " and the first notes also in gold of " Plaisir d'Amour." Another one was a broad gold band, like a wide wedding ring with four hairs attached to it. It could be taken apart and two rings appeared where only one was thought to be.

I was very much attracted by a collection of twelve birthstones, set on a double elephant hair shank. They were presented 12 in a box, or 12 on a white cardboard.

At the top of such cards, his trade-mark was printed. He offered to print some with mine, my name and address in Colombo. That was the way he sold his goods, wholesale, to dealers only, all over the world.

Reluctant to do so, I replied: " Why should I order in Paris Elephant hair jewellery, when I am returning soon to Ceylon where such hair must be available by the handfuls ?"

My good friend Antoine looked at me with a smile of pity, moving slowly his head from side to side, as if I was an innocent and ignorant child.

" How naive ! How refreshing it is to see there are still businessmen like yourself who ' believe ' who are not yet ' blaze.' Why, mon cher ami, don't you know that the Turkish carpets carried by Genuine Arabs, on their shoulder and sold from cafe to cafe, in Cairo, Port Said, and even in Paris, are made in Roubaix and Tourcoing ? That Indian ivory comes from Africa ; Spanish shawls from Canton, Egyptian mummies bracelets from Pfortzeim and even French girls from white Russia ? "

I replied, hotly, aggressively: " You bum ! Do you think that ' we ' are still savages living in the jungle in Ceylon ? "

" Oh no !" protested Antoine, " I know you are very clever, and very capable in the Far East. I am convinced of it, but you also know that the most beautiful girl in the world can only give what she has, don't you ? "

. . . ?

" Well, you simply haven't got it, my friend. "

" What ? The girl ? "

" No, the hair ! "

" We haven't got any elephant hair in Ceylon ? Why, do you imagine that the Ceylon elephant is bald ? or hairless ? "

" Never mind, " replied Antoine with a sarcastic—or was it mysterious-smile.

I left his shop, furious . . .

. . . and came back to peaceful Ceylon.

I was hardly back in harness, when, on a certain morning I received the visit of a commercial traveller. He pulled a long zip and opened his sample bag. Out came milk-white cards, with a gilt edge, upon which were sewed one dozen of . . . elephant hair rings.

" What is that ? " I asked bewildered.

" That is our latest creation; the elephant hair jewellery. Our firm manufactures it exclusively, in Siam. "

This statement—or lie—put me in a joyous and mischievous mood. I started joking : " What do you mean ? Made in Siam ? That is the country of the white elephant . . . and these are black."

" I suppose there is a small village near Paris, called Siam, and that is why they are made in Siam, France ? "

He gave no reply.

" You are a wise man ! This much you have assimilated of oriental wisdom, that you can keep quiet and utter no reply, when caught with a lie. "

We both smiled and had a drink.

" You are in a happy mood, " said the salesman.

" I am always amused when fellows like you come along and, quite seriously, tell me a cock and bull story in which, most of the time, they believe themselves. "

. . .

. . . ? said I

. . . ! said he

About two years later, as I was again getting ready for a short holiday in France, I started collecting a few presents for my people and my friends in Paris.

I bought a few Ceylon gems, really and truly mined in Ratnapura, a few pearls from the Gulf of Mannar, gold filigree articles from Jaffna and Kandyan silverware. All genuinely made in Ceylon, and not in Timbuktu. I knew better now . . .

When, on my list, I came to my friend Antoine, I thought the best present for him would be some raw material for his trade, and I bought him a splendid black elephant tail with at least two hundred strong and long hairs. I wrapped it carefully with plenty of tissue paper and had a special shaped wooden box made to contain it.

Soon after my arrival in Paris I went to Antoine's shop and gave him his present. He opened the box, unwrapped the article and looked at it in mute surprise.

At last he looked up at me and inquired :

" Is this a trophy you brought back from big game hunting in your jungle ? "

" What if it is, " said I offended.

" Well it is not as useful as a pair of horns upon which we could, at least, hang our hat—but, this . . . it is like a miniature and useless broom. "

I was vexed to say the least. I had carried this carefully selected present across fifteen thousand miles of oceans and brought it at my friend's doorstep, to hear him ask me :

" What do you want me to do with *this* ? "

" Elephant hair jewellery, of course. "

" I was afraid of that, replied Antoine. "

From under the counter, he pulled open a large drawer and took out an armful of black spiraled sheep horns.

"Here," he said, "these are the elephant hairs I use for my trade and here is the reason why." He took one of the hairs from the tail I had brought and gave it a three-quarter circle twist. It broke.

" They are brittle. No ring could be made with them. I am really sorry for all the trouble you took on my behalf, but you could not expect me to disclose the secret of my business when I first showed you this new kind of jewellery. Don't you see ? "

. . . ! ! ! said I.

WHAT NOT TO DO

A rich American lady went to Antwerp as she knew it was the proper market to buy loose diamonds, in parcels, from the wholesale trade. But she did not go to the reputable firms of diamond merchants. Instead, she asked a broker to supply her with the stones. In all, she bought for sixty thousand dollars of loose diamonds in the privacy of her hotel room, where the broker brought the goods for her inspection.

That quantity does not take much room and all the lots could easily be concealed in her luggage. It was her intention to do so and smuggle them in the U.S.A., as the duty on diamonds, " back home " was very high.

She asked her broker to recommend her a saddler who could make her a small valise with some sort of secret compartment. He recommended an artisan who's speciality was just that, and who worked alone in his garret.

" Poor man," she thought, " how can he make a living out of this ?"

The job was soon done and discreetly delivered to her. It was impossible to detect the secret compartment and the lady was very satisfied.

With all her luggage safely stored in her cabin she soon reached her destination.

After passport examination, she landed and passed through the Customs.

" Have you anything to declare," she was asked.

" No, absolutely nothing," she replied.

" Please open this bag."

She did so, most confidently.

The Customs Officer went straight for the " secret " compartment and found the diamond parcels at once. The poor lady was amazed at the officers cleverness to detect such specially secret cache.

Of course, the saddler who made the grip was not a " poor man " making his living with his speciality in secret compartments " guaranteed undetectable," but by betraying his customers to the Customs Authorities, who paid him handsomely for each case and particularly in this one, where 60.000 dollars in diamonds were found.

The lady paid a fine of about that amount, to avoid confiscation. One-third of it went to the " poor man."

The beauty of this lesson is that a second-third was paid to the broker who made it also his " speciality " to " finger " his customers to the same Authorities. The moment her passport had revealed her name, all was soon over.

The morality is left to you, to think over.

BIRTHDAY GEMS

What They Signify

Month	Gem	Signifies
January	Garnet or Cinnamon Stone	Fidelity
February	Amethyst	Sincerity
March	Blood Stone or Alexandrite	Courage
April	Diamond	Innocence
May	Emerald or Jade	Wisdom
June	Agate or Cat's Eye	Constancy
July	Ruby	Nobility
August	Zircon or Tourmaline	Virtue
September	Sapphire	Prosperity
October	Opal	Happy Dreams
November	Topaz or Aquamarine	True Love
December	Turquoise or Star Stone	Success

LES GEMMES

Le SAPHIR ETOILE—le bleu du firmament—
Est comme un astérisque au bas d'un testament.
L'AMETHYSTE, au velours teinté du mauve Evêque
Quelque tois lilas pâle ou rouge de pastèque,
LA TOPAZE—au poignard d'un farouche Hidalgo,
Jaune, dorée, orange ou couleur de mango,
RUBIS BALAIS, rouquin, teinté de cinnamone
Qui change le Destin de celui qui le donne,
L'orgueil du SAPHIR BLEU, pour le Mal, pour le Bien,
A outrance toujours, car il est Saturnien,
Pierre aux Vingt Coloris, l'Ardente Tourmaline ,
Electrique et souvent contient deux couleurs fines,
Et le CHRYSO-BERYL, vert amande le jour
Est une Alexandritte, rouge, la nuit—toujours—
LE BERYL, rose ou vert, pierre de la Marine,
Car lorsqu'il tourne au bleu, c'est une aigue-marine,
Et le GRENAT, si beau, mais de peu de valeur
Car il ne peut tenter l'intérêt d'un voleur,
RUBIS—sang de pigeon, dont la pourpre royale,
Avec orgneil impose une frayeur fatale,
L'EMERAUDE, Trésor parmi tous les Trésors,
Dont le vert tranche mieux lorsque serti dans l'or,
La RUTILE a des feux qui la rend si brillante
Que nous avons forgé le mot : " LA RUTILANTE "
LE SPINEL, rouge ou bleu, que souvent l'on a pris
Soit pour un saphir bleu, tantôt pour un Rubis,
Quand le BERYL est mauve il est la Morganite,
Et chaque coloris a son nom par la suite,
LE RUBIS, l'EMERAUDE et non le DIAMANT
Sont les plus précieux, je l'affirme souvent.
Mais, je dois proclamer, les plus belles des gemmes,
Ne valent pas le coeur de la femme que j'aime . . .

SAINT ANDREW'S DAY

TO-NIGHT, 30th November. It is St. Andrew's day, the Patron Saint of Scots. That day is celebrated in the whole world, wherever Scotsmen meet.

To-night, I remember . . .

It was about thirty years ago, I was living in Rangoon, Burma. The country of dagobas, pagodas, rubies and paludism. Not speaking of Cheroots, except that those smoked by women are the size of lamp glasses.

It is also the land where women work and men sleep or make love. I like the Burmese people and that beautiful country. I like the cleanliness and spotless silk dresses of both sexes, their equal temper, their malicious faces, their sweet names and their innumerable wild orchids. It certainly is the Land of Colour.

I was there to buy rubies, mined in Mogog, beyond the untrampable virgin jungle. Brokers, lapidaries and gemmers used to come to Rangoon on regular trips and submit to me the stones they had mined or bought.

I examined them all, made my selection, if any good one was among them and bought it for cash then and there.

That was at the Minto-Mansions, the luxurious Hotel where I lived, just outside the town. At the Hotel bar, I have often bought a fine specimen of Burma ruby, between two whisky-sodas. Brokers came there to see me.

I must say here that if a Burma ruby has really the pigeon blood colour, well known to us, and if it is perfectly pure, it is worth much more than a diamond.

One day a gem broker showed me among other stones, a most beautiful one, weighing five carats. He asked a King's ransom for it. And it was worth it, if I may say that, without humour, being a republican. I lost no time in buying it. I drank a brandy to recover from the joyous shock of surprise I felt, when I found that precious stone mixed with others. Really fine gems are so rare ! I gave him my cheque and let him go. These pigeon blood rubies are usually of a small size, about two or three carats only, and difficult to get. You may count on the fingers of one hand those weighing five carats.

Discretion is almost as difficult to find, in the Far East. The news of my purchase was rapidly grapevined through the hotel and before lunch time, was known to everybody.

A group of rich Scotsmen entered the Bar. They were well known to me. We had a few drinks together.

" ....This calls for a celebration, I said.

We were six in all. That means six rounds of whisky and soda, served rapidly as Scots use to take them. The dose for adults—neat and a few drops of water to rinse the mouth and spit it out under the table. Water should not be swallowed. It is the cause of rust. They drink whisky as we drink wine in France and call it " Mother's milk."

" ....Laddie, you are not the only one, to celebrate. There will be three hundred of us, here, to-night. "

" ....For a fight ? Where ? With whom ? "

They looked at me, puzzled.

" ....Poor Froggy ! Has your mother forgotten to tell you that St. Andrew's day falls on the 30th of November ? "

With a fat forefinger, one of them pointed, dramatically, towards the hotel park, clearly visible through the window of the bar :

" ....Do you hear the noise of hammers ? "

I assumed an air of melodrama :

" ....I hear it. Great Scot ! Who are they going to decapitate or hang ? "

" ....Shut up, Froggy ! This is serious business. "

" ....I should say so ! Three hundred dinners at Rs. 10/- per head, totals Rs. 3,000/-. "

They all pitied my ignorance.

" ....A huge table is being constructed, horse shoe shaped, for our annual St. Andrew's day. To-night at 9.30. Strictly Scot and kilt."

Jokingly, I added, " Is it not a kind of skirt, worn in your country, by old gentlemen, more or less whiskered and with long moustaches ? "

" ....Stop it, Laddie. A kilt is not a skirt. It requires thirty yards of the finest Scot woollen tweed to make one."

" ....I agree with you, " I said, " it is serious business. "

" ....Your ignorance is revolting. We will show you, to-night."

" ....Am I going to be among you as the 301st ? "

" ....No, you will be the only non-Scot. "

" ....I certainly accept your invitation with enthusiasm. "

Whereupon six other drinks were served. The same adults' doses and pretty soon we started singing highland songs.

From time to time, one of them, repeated :

" ....We are going to show you, to-night. "

I was also reminded to bring my own bottle of whisky. " One and individual," I thought. Am I already drunk ? I am afraid it is so.

Timidly, I protested against the strong and stiff quantity of liquor they made me take.

Before one glass was quite emptied, another one was placed on the table.

One of my friends took a box of matches out of his pocket and placed it flat on the table, against his glass.

" ....This is the quantity for a Froggy."

I approved. It seemed quite enough for me.

" This is what an Englishman takes " ; and he put the box on its side.

" Here is what a Scotsman drinks "; this time he put the box straight up. " A Scot may not take . . ."

" ....More than that ? "

" ....No, He may not take less. "

" ....Well, I'll be damned. "

" These Froggies," said one to the others, " have yet a lot to learn, don't you think ? "

I smiled, good humouredly and let the remark pass. They all approved with a nod of the head. Six other whiskies were served.

Again ! I had enough ! I am not trained for that kind of " serious business." I took English leave as we say in French. I was in need of my usual nap. I had to take a good nap, if I wished to look refreshed, that evening at the banquet. I locked my precious ruby in the safe and ordered my bottle of whisky.

I went to bed. The blinds of my room, were down, and the light filtering through them made a black and white zebra pattern on the white washed walls. Within a few minutes, I was in the arms of Morphius. At about eight o'clock, I got up, washed, shaved and dressed with the meticulous care I always took with my toilet.

To honour my hosts, I had put on a Scotch tie, with large red, green and yellow squares.

I went down to the hotel lobby. Many guests had already arrived. The exhibition of colours was generous and also blinding. My first impression was that they were already somewhat drunk. They all had a glass in one hand and the whisky bottle in the other. I thought to myself :

" The Knights of the Glass." I mixed with the crowd and got drowned in it.

In spite of my latin type, one of the Scots asked :

" Are you Mac-Intosh or Mac-Intyre ? "

I lifted my tie up with one finger and replied " Mac Farlane."

It was the name I found upon the label attached to my tie when I bought it that same day. This deception or " make believe " was necessary, as long as I had not found my five friends. All of a sudden, I saw them coming in and I joined them. They were followed by a dozen others, all wearing the kilt and the paraphernalia that goes with it, even the " dirk " dagger, surmounted by a golden cairngorm on the handle, and carried in the stocking at the height of the knee. Each one of the twelve had his bag pipe under the arm ready to start playing.

Martial and serene they placed themselves in Indian file, one behind the other, and were ready to start turning around our large shoe horse-shaped table and play. They will be playing and turning during the whole dinner, until the majority of the guests will be sleeping, their nose inside their plates or lying under the table, until daybreak.

My host happened to be the Chairman of this Assembly. He honoured me by making me sit at his right. All of us had our full bottle of whisky in front.

A monstrously loud guttural word, sounding like "Hoch," was uttered with one voice, by the whole assembly and we all sat down to dine. The Chairman stood up for his speech of welcome to his countrymen, as he did every year, on St. Andrew's day. The pipers stopped turning and playing.

Before giving his speech in Gaelic, he investigated the solidity of his chair, then placed one foot on it, the other upon the table. We usually say that Spanish and Dutch are guttural languages. Have you ever heard a Scot speaking Gaelic ? That is the top. To me it seemed that he was gargling with pebbles.

His address was brief. I thought he had said plenty in a few words, or else he must have been fearful that his chair might collapse under his tremendous weight. It could also have been that, quite naturally, he was hungry or most probably thirsty.

Another "Hoch" was shouted in unison and they all began eating and drinking. The pipers started turning around the table and the strident notes of the clans tore the air with a certain majesty.

At least, that is the impression I gathered at the moment because I had already taken a few " adults' doses " and I was not quite certain if it was the pipers who were turning around us or if it was I who was turning around them.

I looked at the menu. It was an enormous selection of fine food. Almost Gargantuesc or Pantagruelic. It was written in French of course, just to make you believe that the cooking was French. Which, in fact, it was, the Hotel cook being my friend, Monsieur Leclerc.

An inspiration came to the Chairman and it threw him out of his chair. Again he uttered some guttural sounds above the cacophonic noises of the whole table. The result of this was that all the eyes fell upon me, speculatively and intrigued. My speech was demanded by all, whether I liked it or not.

I was given only a few seconds to recover from my surprise but I was not allowed to avoid making a speech. Some giant hands caught me under the arms and I was put right in the centre of the table, between the glasses and bottles.

Calling forth all my remaining rhetoric, I started my speech by an *Exorde Ex-Abrupto*, charging head first, into my subject. I had to make use, as you can easily imagine, of all the wind I had left in my lungs, to be heard by such a large gathering.

" Do you know that Mary, Queen of Scots, was a Queen of France ? "

Replics came from everywhere :

" Yes, no, yes, no."

" . . . and that the Scotch Laird who married her later, was the brother-in-law of a defunct King of France ? "

" Yes, no, yes, no."
The attentive assembly seemed puzzled.

" I see that opinions are very divided, therefore, I propose— to make it short—that those who know it, instruct those who don't."

This joke was enough to result in a huge explosion of laughter. After that, I babbled upon the *Entente Cordiale,* which was an actuality, at the time. The fumes of the whisky I had ingurgitated mounted rapidly to my brain and with the remnants of whatever coherence I still possessed, I spoke yet a little more and still a little more.

I was of that type of speaker whom you have to beg and beg to make them speak and once they get started they have to be shot dead to make them shut up.

I cannot recollect what I said after that. I only remember my last word as well as my last gesture. They are still vividly imprinted in my memory.

I bent to take my glass, lying at the tip of my shoes and I lifted it high, giving my hosts their national Gaelic toast : " S'shlan-zivarl."

Three hundred pairs of powerful lungs joined in and repeated after me, " S'shlanzivarl."

In one gulp, I emptied my glass and threw it violently above my shoulder at the foot of a palm tree, where it broke in a hundred pieces.

And I suddenly disappeared under the table . . . exhausted and drunk.

. . . .or almost that !

Now, this story should have ended here, and there would have been little harm done. Unfortunately it was not to be so.

The story continues. . . .

And here it is.

The next morning the room-boy brings me in bed, as usual, my chotta hazri, composed of strong black coffee and a fruit. I adopt a sitting position to hold the tray on my knees while I scratch my aching head. There is pain behind my eyes, pain on the surface of my scalp and other kinds of pain,—all different—in my mouth and my muscles, all over my body. I feel as if I had been beaten up or drummed upon. My stomach has revolted and is crying it aloud.

The morning light is blinding my poor eyes. While I sip a little coffee, from the corner of my eyes, I see a square of white paper and I smile, tender hearted. Looking up, it seems to me that I can read, on the boy's face, the kind of smile I would expect from an accomplice.

....The son of a gun ! I think to myself.

And aloud, I ask him, moaning mildly :

" ....Who is the lady . . . this time ? "

A quick mental gymnastic and I think I guessed who she is. I mean, which one.

Pityless, the boy drops from his full height : " It is the Manager, Sir."

What ? The Hotel Director ? What does he want of me ? At this early hour when the crows have hardly been awake ? What is the cause of this hurry ? All these questions come to my mind and I cannot answer them. He is a French Swiss, a good old friend of mine. We often drink and joke together.

" ....Well, ask him in."

He enters my room with a cordial smile and his hand outstretched.

...." Congratulations, my dear friend, bravo! You were superb last night."

I smell a rat and become cautious. He has no pity in his make up. He starts again :

" Bravo! Very good! Of course, I am not at all surprised. I know you are an ancient pupil of Maurice de Feraudy of the Comedie Francaise, and the " Eloquence of Gesture " which you displayed yesterday, was entirely in the Tradition of the House. How I like and appreciate it you cannot imagine. Your success was complete ! "

The rat I was smelling was probably a musk rat. The odour betrays him. This avalanche of praising is some sort of hidden trap. I am certainly going to get something in the neck.

" Now, what is it you are driving at ? "

He points to the white square of paper on my tray.

" I have expressed my admiration upon that scrap of paper."

I snatched it and read an amount :—Thirty rupees.—

" Why do you make such a loud story for thirty rupees, I cannot imagine. You can charge it to my bill, if you like. I don't care. In any case, let me remind you that I was their guest and if I have to pay for my Scotch friend's invitation it does not surprise me at all, but I am prepared to pay and keep quiet."

" ....Dear Monsieur," he replied sarcastically, " I fear you are still a little asleep or not quite awake. Have a second look.—Close.—

" ....What ? Three hundred rupees ?"

...." Yes, Sir, three hundred rupees only. Errors and omissions excepted. Your *Ultima Verba* was splendid and was worthy of the great actor your old Master was. But . . . "

...." . . . But what ? "

...." But why did you have the unlucky idea to hurl your glass above your shoulder after your speech ? "

" . . . . . . ?? "

...." I have charged you only one rupee per glass."

" . . . . . . ? "

" ....Of course ! All the guests have thrown theirs the same way, after yours ! "

The profit I made on that ruby covered this unforeseen expense.

What kind of a Scotch " invitation " was that ?